CW00544804

OFFICES

BY ETHAN COEN

★

★

DRAMATISTS
PLAY SERVICE
INC.

OFFICES
Copyright © 2010, Ethan Coen

All Rights Reserved

SPECIAL NOTE

Anyone receiving permission to produce any or all of the Plays in the volume OFFICES is required to give credit to the Author as sole and exclusive Author of the Play(s) on the title page of all programs distributed in connection with performances of the Play(s) and in all instances in which the title(s) of the Play(s) appears for purposes of advertising, publicizing or otherwise exploiting the Play(s) and/or a production thereof. The name of the Author must appear on a separate line, in which no other name appears, immediately beneath the title(s) and in size of type equal to 50% of the size of the largest, most prominent letter used for the title(s) of the Play(s). No person, firm or entity may receive credit larger or more prominent than that accorded the Author. The following acknowledgment must appear on the title page in all programs distributed in connection with performances of the Play(s):

World Premiere
Presented By
Atlantic Theatre Company
New York City, 2009

OFFICES received its world premiere Off-Broadway at the Atlantic Theater, opening on May 9, 2009. It was directed by Neil Pepe; the set design was by Riccardo Hernandez; the costume design was by Laura Bauer; the lighting design was by David Weiner; the original music and sound design were by Obadiah Eaves; and the stage manager was Alison DeSantis. The cast was as follows:

PEER REVIEW

ELLIOTT	Joey Slotnick
LAURA	Aya Cash
MARK	Daniel Abeles
CARL	C.J. Wilson
CASSADY	F. Murray Abraham

HOMELAND SECURITY

LOUIE	Daniel Abeles
INVESTIGATOR	Brennan Brown
EMMA/SECRETARY	Aya Cash
MUNRO	John Bedford Lloyd
BRAD	Greg Stuhr
WILSON	C.J. Wilson
BOBBY	Daniel Yelsky
JUDY	Mary McCann

STRUGGLE SESSION

BUM	F. Murray Abraham
SECOND COLLEAGUE	Brennan Brown
LURY	John Bedford Lloyd
BECK	Daniel London
COLLEAGUE	Joey Slotnick
SCHILLING	Greg Stuhr
THIRD COLLEAGUE	C.J. Wilson

OFFICES

PEER REVIEW

CHARACTERS

ELLIOTT

LAURA

MARK

CARL

CASSADY

All the characters except Cassady are youngish — on either side of thirty.

PEER REVIEW

Scene 1

An office.

Laura sits very still at her desk, gazing off with a faint smile.

A long beat.

The door swings open and Elliot bustles in, furiously flipping through papers.

ELLIOT. Have you seen this shit!
LAURA. What shit.
ELLIOT. This peer review shit, have you seen it?
LAURA. Nuh-uh.
ELLIOT. What a bunch of goddamn shit!
LAURA. Really?
ELLIOT. Oh my god!
LAURA. Yeah?
ELLIOT. Oh my god! You should see this! *(Handing her the papers.)* *Look* at this shit!
LAURA. *(Flipping through.)* Wow ... Wow ... *I* did okay ...
ELLIOT. Did you?
LAURA. Uh-huh.
ELLIOT. I got slagged off like you wouldn't believe.
LAURA. Mm.
ELLIOT. Somebody ripped me, big time.
LAURA. Boy, Mark did good.
ELLIOT. Huh-yeah. Mark did great.
LAURA. Wow.
ELLIOT. What a fucking joke. This "peer review" shit is just like a,

like a, like score-settling, like anonymously denouncing, you know ...

LAURA. Uh-huh.

ELLIOT. Whatever. The whole process is doomed to be fucked.

LAURA. Boy — Mark did good.

ELLIOT. That's why this company is fucked.

LAURA. You think?

ELLIOT. It pretends to be human. You know. Concerned with what the "worker-owners" think. Et cetera.

LAURA. Right.

ELLIOT. Which is a tool. To turn us into, you know, willing accomplices. Like in East Germany.

LAURA. Whuh.

ELLIOT. Well like in East Germany ninety percent of the population was police informers. Like you had informers informing on informers, and the other ten percent basically sorting it out. Like something like forty percent of the gross national product was dossiers.

LAURA. God. *(Beat.)* Forty percent?

ELLIOT. Shit, I don't know, but, I mean, a lot.

LAURA. Wow.

ELLIOT. And this is the same. "Peer review."

LAURA. Well, Elliot ... Every system has winners and losers. *(Beat.)*

ELLIOT. Winners and losers!

LAURA. Uh-huh.

ELLIOT. Well yes every system has winners and losers — the question is is it fair? Does it figure it out right, assign it right. Fucking *shit!*

LAURA. Mm.

ELLIOT. *Should* A win or lose, *should* B; elementary, you know, *should* they!

LAURA. Okay.

ELLIOT. Ah forget it. You know what, if you see Cassady, if Cassady wants to talk to me about this, just tell him to go fuck himself. *(Beat.)*

LAURA. Those words?

ELLIOT. Those — no, forget it, I'm just ... forget it ... *(He is leaving. Laura waves the papers after him.)*

LAURA. You want these? *(The door slams. A quiet beat. Laura pushes her castered chair back from her desk and, by her body move-*

ment, appears to be tugging down the hem of her skirt. Mark emerges from her side of the desk, having been in the legwell. He stands.)

MARK. God, what a loser.

LAURA. Who — Elliot?

MARK. Yeah. Christ's sake. *(Absently wipes his mouth and chin with his sleeve.)* Talk about sour grapes. Lemme see. *(She hands him the papers. A beat.)* I did do pretty good.

Scene 2

Carl's office.

Elliot lectures Carl, who sits at his desk.

ELLIOT. A whole system, see? It's not like, it's not like, you know. I'm not some raving conspiracy theorist. I'm not saying a bunch of people met in a dark room to figure this out. This is just how the system grew. Over time. To meet the company's needs.

CARL. Uh-huh.

ELLIOT. It's not *our* needs. I mean it takes into *account* our needs, but only to figure out how best, you know, to exploit us. The organism adapts. It figures out different ways how best to use us. Not in a dark room. Not late at night with, you know, lowered voices and shit. But, like, these delusory stock options, you know, to keep us docile —

CARL. Delusory?

ELLIOT. When're *you* gonna get vested? You know? Are you ever gonna see that shit?

CARL. Uh-huh.

ELLIOT. Not fucking likely. Any time soon. Any time ever. And so this company organism, you know, oozes over us, traveling on its own slime trail, creeping up on us and engulfing us so we're covered in company slime and doing company bidding.

CARL. God.

ELLIOT. Robbed of our will. Because the slime has oozed into us and replaced our will with company will. We internalize the slime.

11

(Beat.)

CARL. And you think that's fucked.

ELLIOT. Yes that's fucked! What do *you* think! *(Beat.)*

CARL. I guess it's fucked.

ELLIOT. Fuckin' A!

CARL. Uh-huh.

ELLIOT. Do you understand what I'm saying? About brainwashing, in a democracy? You think a democracy doesn't brainwash? You think it's only totalitarian models?

CARL. I don't know.

ELLIOT. Wake up, man! Smell the coffee! We all want to fit in. Sure! They count on that! And so they use us all to pressure each other to want to fit in more! Good Germans! Hitler was *elected*, you know.

CARL. To what? *(Beat.)*

ELLIOT. To — head of — Germany!

CARL. Okay. *(Beat.)*

ELLIOT. *Get* it?

CARL. I knew he was head of Germany. *(Beat.)*

ELLIOT. So are you with me, will you help? On this "peer review" thing? Add your voice?

CARL. Not right now.

ELLIOT. *(Nodding.)* Not right now. Okay. *(Beat.)* Stooge. *(Striding to the door.)* Asshole stooge fucker. Fuck you. *(He slams the door. A very long beat. Carl is staring off with a faint smile and a faraway look.)*

CARL. Oh, man.

Scene 3

Cassady is perched on his desk facing Elliot, standing.

A long beat. They gaze at each other.

ELLIOT. Bothering people.

CASSADY. Yes.

ELLIOT. Who says.

CASSADY. The people you've been bothering.

ELLIOT. Who says. *Who.*

CASSADY. Names?

ELLIOT. Uh-huh.

CASSADY. No.

ELLIOT. No? What no.

CASSADY. Names? So that you can harass them more? No.

ELLIOT. I haven't been harassing anyone. Bothering anyone. I think maybe I've opened some eyes.

CASSADY. Uh-huh.

ELLIOT. And this is why you're afraid, maybe.

CASSADY. Afraid.

ELLIOT. Yep.

CASSADY. I'm afraid.

ELLIOT. What would you call it? *(Beat.)*

CASSADY. Unafraid.

ELLIOT. Oh. Oh really. So why am I here. Kafka.

CASSADY. Because you've been bothering people.

ELLIOT. Oh really. Suppose you tell me —

CASSADY. And please don't call me Kafka.

ELLIOT. You know why I call you Kafka?

CASSADY. Yes I know why you call me Kafka.

ELLIOT. How come. Why do I c —

CASSADY. Because he wrote those books. Little men. Put-upon. By institutions. Nameless tormentors. But "Kafka" is the name of the writer. You should call me "Nameless Tormentor." *(Beat)* Or whatever. But not "Kafka."

ELLIOT. Fine. Is this your point? *I* think the point here is —

CASSADY. The point is you're fucking pestering people. And bringing them down. By revealing to them — what, that the company wants to get the most out of them? Possible? You just figured this out? Einstein?

ELLIOT. Well, but there's a nefarious ... um ... *(Beat.)*

CASSADY. What.

ELLIOT. There's stuff that I think even you aren't aware of. Because it's institutionalized. Built in.

CASSADY. What. *(Beat.)*

ELLIOT. Well — I — I — I —

CASSADY. And this is why your peer review was so poor. Because

13

you natter and annoy.

ELLIOT. What do you want me to do! Cassady! Pretend everything's all right? Suck up for the peer review, suck everyone's dicks? *(Beat.)*

CASSADY. That's your business.

Scene 4

Laura's office again.

ELLIOT. Just keeping everyone docile, you know. That's their agenda. And they enlist us in that. Without saying anything. Without doing anything. But their *in*action, see, speaks volumes.

LAURA. You're pissed off because they're *not* doing anything. *(Beat.)*

ELLIOT. Cheap shot, Laura. Cheap shot.

LAURA. But that's what you're saying.

ELLIOT. Are you on their side? Buying into their shit?

LAURA. Why is it us/them? Why do you have to be angry all the time? And unhappy? Why can't you just do your work and, you know … *(He stares at her as the speech peters out. At length:)*

ELLIOT. You slagged me off, didn't you.

LAURA. What?

ELLIOT. On the peer review.

LAURA. Elliot —

ELLIOT. I thought we were friends. Or, you know, friendly colleagues. Professional colleague friends. And then it turns out *this*?

LAURA. Elliot —

ELLIOT. So fucked up. So-o-o-o fucked up.

LAURA. Elliot, you're not —

ELLIOT. This is how — this just bears out what I've been saying.

LAURA. Elliot —

ELLIOT. Elliot! Elliot! Elliot! *(Beat.)*

LAURA. *(Quietly.)* I'm sorry you're unhappy. But then you go around trying to make everyone else unhappy. Like water level, you know, trying to make everything else the same level. Is how you operate. *(Beat.)*

ELLIOT. You don't see how *they* operate? How they keep us all happy?

LAURA. You don't want to be happy? *(Long beat. They gaze at each other.)*

Scene 5

Laura, Mark, and Carl stand around a water cooler, holding small paper cones of water, laughing.

Laughter. Laughter for a good long beat.

The door opens. Elliot enters.

The laughter immediately becomes self-conscious. It withers and, as Elliot pulls a paper cone from a dispenser and fills it, dies.

An awkward silence as Elliot's three coworkers shift in silence, unsure of where to look. Carl gazes down at the paper cone he holds, and sighs.

CARL. Well ... *(He tosses back the last bit of water, crumples the cone, drops the cone in the wastebasket, and ambles out the door. More heavy silence; brief throat-clearing from Mark; finally he and Laura leave as well. Elliot is left sipping from his cone, one hand dug into a pocket, frowning at a point in space.)*

Scene 6

Cassady's office.

Once again Cassady, perched on his desk, and Elliot, planted before it, stare at each other for a long beat.

Finally, in a tone of I'm-not-sure-I-heard-you-right:

CASSADY. Where? *(Beat.)*
ELLIOT. Up your goddamn ass. *(Beat.)*
CASSADY. Okay.
ELLIOT. Right up your goddamn ass.
CASSADY. Right. Okay.
ELLIOT. Because I quit.
CASSADY. Gotcha. *(Beat.)*
ELLIOT. That's all you have to say?
CASSADY. Um. Not much to say.
ELLIOT. Not much to say. Three years of loyal service. Three years of my life.
CASSADY. Which I'm supposed to stick up my ass.
ELLIOT. Not the three years of my life. The job.
CASSADY. Okay. You weren't making that distinction.
ELLIOT. This place is so fucked.
CASSADY. Some of us like it. *(Beat.)*
ELLIOT. Okay, fine, forget it. I'll stay.
CASSADY. That's okay.
ELLIOT. What.
CASSADY. You don't have to stay. *(Beat.)*
ELLIOT. Are you fucking firing me?

Scene 7

Laura's office.

She sits at her desk. Elliot is perched upon it.

She stares at him for a beat.

LAURA. I can't believe it. *(Beat.)* How come?
ELLIOT. 'Cause I know how shit works around here. 'Cause I know what's really going on.
LAURA. That's what he said?
ELLIOT. Well no he's not gonna *say* that!
LAURA. Uh-huh.
ELLIOT. I mean, *god.*
LAURA. Uh-huh. Well what *did* he say?
ELLIOT. About ...
LAURA. Why are you fired?
ELLIOT. Well ... hard to say ... hard to say ...
LAURA. Hard to say — what he said?
ELLIOT. Huh?
LAURA. I mean, what did he say? You're fired because ...
ELLIOT. Oh, what the fuck difference does it make what he said!
LAURA. Uh-huh. *(He turns to go.)*
ELLIOT. Ya know? Like I'm really interested in the company line!
(He goes through the door and slams it behind him. Long beat. Laura pushes herself away from the desk and Carl emerges from the legwell. He stands and stretches side-to-side, hands on hips, having been cooped up for some time.)
CARL. Boy. *That* sucks.

Scene 8

Elliot's office.

He stands at his desk, loading the contents of its drawers into a cardboard box that stands open on the desktop.

The door opens and Laura, Carl, and Mark enter.

Elliot stares at them, frozen, hand holding effects arrested halfway to the box.

LAURA. Hi Elliot. *(Beat.)*
ELLIOT. Hi.
CARL. We just wanted to say, um …
LAURA. We just wanted to say, um, to tell you we liked working with you. And that it's so so sad you're going. Seriously. *(Elliot stares at them. Mark steps forward and thrusts out a hand.)*
MARK. Good luck, buddy. *(Elliot allows his hand to be taken and pumped. Mark steps back. A beat.)*
CARL. You were really cool, Elliot. I like, learned so much from you. Your viewpoint was always new and informative and I really learned a ton. Which I'll always carry with me.
LAURA. And you should be proud of that part of yourself. Because that spark within you is —
CARL. It's a really cool thing.
LAURA. It's a really cool thing, and — *(Elliot bursts into tears. Carl, Laura, and Mark look at each other uneasily. At length:)*
LAURA. Elliot —
ELLIOT. You think I give a shit what *you* think! You fuckers! You won't even *do* anything! Who went into Cassady's office and said, No, don't fire Elliot, or I quit! You can't fire Elliot for knowing how things really work around here! Punishing him for, you know! Who said *that?!* *(Starts flinging the rest of his effects into the box.)* Well I don't give a shit! I leave with my head held up high! They didn't get to *me*! To go along! And now you think I give a shit what you fuckers think!

18

You can't even see what's going on! Dopes! *(Continuing to shed tears of rage he slides two hands under the box and hoists it. He goes to the door. Dipping one shoulder, he awkwardly tries to work the knob. As the door rattles in its frame Elliot's three coworkers, heads hung, sneak glances. Finally Carl goes to the door and opens it for him. Elliot exits weeping. Carl sadly closes the door and the three colleagues stand shamefaced as the sobs recede to silence. Long beat of silence. The door explodes open and Elliot reenters, weeping loudly. He marches to his desk, yanks open a drawer, pulls out a stapler, and stomps off, slamming the door behind him. Sobs once again recede to silence. Slow fade.)*

Scene 9

Laura's office.

She sits at her desk reading a newspaper.

Her fists tighten on the paper.

LAURA. Oh my god! *(Scans farther down the page.)* Oh my god! Oh my god! *(Slams the paper down and stares off into space, apparently lost in thought; then:)* Oh my god! Oh my god! OH MY GOD! *(A beat of rigid suspense. A wilting beat. Laura collects herself. Finally, into space:)* Did you see the paper?
MARK. *(Muffled; from legwell.)* This morning?
LAURA. *(Pushing away from desk.)* Yeah. Oh my god! *(Mark emerges. He crooks his head this way and that.)*
MARK. Yeah?
LAURA. Oh my god! Remember Elliot? *(A blank look from Mark.)* Elliot Vogel? He got fired after last year's peer review?
MARK. Oh yeah. That loser.
LAURA. Well there's a review of his book in the paper!
MARK. Oh yeah?
LAURA. Like, a really good review! They say it's really good!
MARK. The book?
LAURA. Yeah!

MARK. Who wrote it? *(Beat.)*
LAURA. The review?
MARK. Elliot's book. *(Beat.)*
LAURA. *El*liot. It's *his book.*
MARK. His *that* way?
LAURA. Yeah, I'm just happening to glance down here —
MARK. Huh.
LAURA. I, I happen to glance down and I notice this review and oh my god, it's all about this *book* by *Elliot!*
MARK. Huh.
LAURA. You know what it's about?
MARK. Huh-uh.
LAURA. There's this family and they live in suburbia and then the son wants to go live in the downtown area. There's tension and stuff and he strikes out on his own and meets like lots of people and then a mysterious friend.
MARK. Boy.
LAURA. A novel. A book. *(Beat.)*
MARK. How many pages?
LAURA. And they say it's like, "not merely a promising work but a work that fully delivers — marshaling, in a first novel, insights his more practiced peers might envy." And praises his writing style and so on and it's like great.
MARK. Wow. Who did he blow to get *that* review. *(Beat.)* And I always thought he was a loser.
LAURA. No. Just artistic. *(Mark laces his fingers above his head and dips first to one side, then the other, stretching.)*
MARK. *(Genuine; generous.)* Well. Good for him … good for him … *(As we start to fade out Mark frowns and works his tongue, feeling something on it. Just before we lose him to black he reaches to his mouth, to pluck.)*

End of Play

HOMELAND SECURITY

CHARACTERS

LOUIE

INVESTIGATOR

EMMA

MUNRO

BRAD

WILSON

BOBBY

JUDY

SECRETARY

HOMELAND SECURITY

Bob Munro is a functionary in the Department of Homeland Security.

There are two sets, Office and Home. Office is a nondescript office. Home is a living room. Both sets are minimal.

At the office are Munro's two colleagues: Brad, somewhat younger, and Wilten, Munro's contemporary.

At home are his wife Judy, teenage daughter Emma, and twelve-year-old son Bobby.

Scene 1

Office.

Brad stands over the shoulder of seated Bob Munro, laying printed pages onto the desk in front of him. Brad waits a beat after depositing each page so that Munro can absorb the information. Munro gazes down, chin cupped in palm, bored.

BRAD. Air … *(Lays down the next page.)* Ensiled grains … *(Next page.)* Water supply … *(Next page.)* Nuclear … *(Next page.)* Other hazmat … *(Next page.)* Ports and Tunnels —
MUNRO. Christ! *(He grabs the page and studies, it, eyes wide. His look drifs to a spot in space. He squints, thinking.)* Where's lunch?
BRAD. Lunch. Good question. *(Looks at his watch.)* Should I call?
MUNRO. The place?
BRAD. Yeah.

MUNRO. Yeah. *(Sets page down.)* It's been what, an hour?

BRAD. Hasn't been an hour.

MUNRO. Wanna bet?

BRAD. Um. An hour?

MUNRO. You bet your bippy.

BRAD. An hour ago we ordered? From right now? Or that it gets here?

MUNRO. It didn't *get* here an hour ago. We know *some* things.

BRAD. So, we ordered. An hour ago. You're saying. Or that it'll have been an hour, once it gets here.

MUNRO. Already has been, I'm saying. So it will have been, yes. Already has been is the bet.

BRAD. And we're betting…?

MUNRO. Lunch.

BRAD. A*bout* lunch.

MUNRO. And *betting* lunch. Lunch is the bet. Loser buys lunch. *(Wilten enters.)*

WILTEN. Where's lunch. It's been like an hour.

MUNRO. See?

BRAD. Yeah but — but —

MUNRO. But that's not probative?

WILTEN. What's the deal with Ports and Tunnels.

MUNRO. Scary stuff. Brad is buying lunch.

BRAD. But that's not probative, Wilten saying —

MUNRO. *(Mocking.)* "That's not probative." What're you, a god-damn lawyer?

WILTEN. Hostile workplace.

MUNRO. My ass. *(A buzz. Projecting toward phone:)* In a meeting!

SECRETARY. *(Through phone.)* Okay, but —

MUNRO. In a meeting! Did you not hear me!

SECRETARY. I'm sorry, sir.

MUNRO. She's sorry. These people. *(Munro sorts one-by-one through the papers Brad brought in, forming three piles on his desk.)* Shred. Shred. Act. Shred. File. Act. Shhhhhhhhhred. *(He leans back. He leans forward again and plucks the top sheet off the Shred pile.)* No, Act.

WILTEN. Just had a thought.

MUNRO. Uh-huh?

WILTEN. *(Indicating phone.)* What if that was lunch. *(The three men freeze, staring at the phone. At length Munro leans cautiously in and hits a button.)*

MUNRO. Dolores?

SECRETARY. Yes sir.

MUNRO. Was that … lunch?

SECRETARY. No sir, the undersecretary.

MUNRO. … *The* undersecretary?

SECRETARY. Yes sir. He said it was important.

MUNRO. Okay. *(He leans back, relaxing. He leans to the phone again with a thought.)* Said *what* was important.

SECRETARY. Didn't say, sir.

MUNRO. Okay. *(Leans back.)* Then, it can't be that important. *(Forward again to phone.)* Call me when lunch gets here. *(Brad scoops the three piles off the desktop, messily conflating.)*

BRAD. So none of these were Act?

Scene 2

Home.

Munro stands planted, hands on hips. He looks one way. He looks the other way.

MUNRO. Emma?

EMMA. *(Off.)* Yes, Dad.

MUNRO. Where's my briefcase?

EMMA. *(Entering.)* Gee, I haven't been tracking that, Dad.

MUNRO. Very amusing. Every day I come home you know where I put it?

EMMA. Uh …

MUNRO. The hall closet. Every day in the hall closet, always in the same place.

EMMA. That is so interesting, Dad.

MUNRO. So I can find it.

EMMA. Wow, Dad. Really.

MUNRO. So I know where it is.

EMMA. Yeah, okay. Good thinking.

MUNRO. But it's not there.

EMMA. Oh no. What can *I* do to help.

MUNRO. You know there's classified stuff in there. Important stuff. I'm not talking about old newspapers and a spare sweater. Though there's that, too. (*To his wife, entering.*) Honey? Have you seen my briefcase?

JUDY. Ask Emma.

EMMA. Mom, I'm busy photographing some files. To sell to the Russians.

MUNRO. Very amusing. We're not really worried about the Russians any more, dear. Our enemy now wears a kaffiyeh. Or brandishes an assegai. And you know this sarcasm, which seems to be the only tool in your toolbelt, someday you'll learn that sarcasm is not the appropriate response to every single thing everyone says to you.

EMMA. Boy, Dad, I look forward to learning that. I bet it'll make me a better person.

JUDY. Why bring the briefcase home. You always leave it in the closet and watch the baseball game.

MUNRO. Yes but *knowing* there's work I should be doing helps me enjoy the ballgame more intensely.

JUDY. So before the ballgame starts, we're supposed to run around and help you find the briefcase so you can ignore it.

MUNRO. It's not just a question of my state of mind. I'm not a raving narcissist. There are sensitive materials in that briefcase. Materials that, in the wrong hands — has Louie been here?

EMMA. He's coming over now.

MUNRO. I don't like Louie.

EMMA. He likes you. I don't know why.

JUDY. I don't either.

MUNRO. Nor I. I don't trust it.

JUDY. Louie is very sweet.

MUNRO. This, I think, is what dooms him.

EMMA. Dooms him? To what?

MUNRO. Selling soft yogurt at the mall for the rest of his life.

JUDY. Soft *ice* cream.

EMMA. Yogurt is always soft.

MUNRO. Oh — it's soft *ice* cream.

EMMA. Uh-huh.

MUNRO. *Not* yogurt.

EMMA. No.

MUNRO. I've been underestimating that boy.

EMMA. So, this is like ten seconds after you lecture me about sarcasm?

MUNRO. Yeah, see, the difference is, I use it selectively.

LOUIE. Hi Emma.

EMMA. Hi Louie.

MUNRO. What?! Where did you come from? How much of that did you overhear?

LOUIE. How much of what.

MUNRO. How much of — you're not being clever, are you?

LOUIE. Clever?

MUNRO. How did you get in here?

LOUIE. My key.

MUNRO. Your key.

LOUIE. Emma gave me a key.

EMMA. Dad, he comes here like all the time.

MUNRO. So you're handing out keys to the place? Is everyone handing out keys? Question: wouldn't it be easier to take the lock off the front door? Or remove the door altogether?

EMMA. Dad, let's not be paranoid. I gave a key to Louie.

LOUIE. I could give it back, sir. If it's a problem.

MUNRO. All right, let's just pause here and try to put all the pieces together. My briefcase is missing. Louie has a key to the house. *(Beat.)*

EMMA. That's two pieces.

MUNRO. Sometimes you only need two pieces. Walk the cat backward. You need more pieces?

LOUIE. I could return it, sir.

MUNRO. The key? Or the briefcase?

LOUIE. What briefcase.

MUNRO. Laughably easy of course, feigning ignorance.

LOUIE. *(To Emma.)* Does he want me to give the key back?

EMMA. He doesn't know what he wants.

MUNRO. *Who* doesn't. *I* do. *Who* doesn't.

LOUIE. What's walking the cat backwards?

EMMA. I dunno. What's an assegai.

LOUIE. A what?

MUNRO. An assegai.

JUDY. The baseball game is on.

MUNRO. A curved sword. Does anyone know where my briefcase is? Am I speaking a foreign language here?

LOUIE. No.

MUNRO. Am I the only sane person in this room?

JUDY. Not even if you were alone.

LOUIE. Sir, are you uncomfortable with me?

MUNRO. I'm uncomfortable. Part of it is you.

JUDY. The baseball game is on. If you're not going to watch it, why did you lug that briefcase home? *(Munro stares at her, thinking.)*

MUNRO. *Did* I bring it home today?

Scene 3

Office.

Munro is leaning back, feet on his desk. Wilten leans against the doorjamb, hands thrust into his pockets.

WILTEN. Just can't seem to pull the trigger.

MUNRO. Not a good reason to keep things going.

WILTEN. No. Although I like her. Sometimes. Sometimes I like her. I, you know, I enjoy her.

MUNRO. Uh-huh.

WILTEN. Her legs bend back.

MUNRO. Uh-huh.

WILTEN. But she's so damned needy.

MUNRO. Mm.

WILTEN. Last summer, Fourth of July weekend. I tell her I'm going out for a drink. Well my cell phone starts ringing. "What's taking you, baby, I miss you. When're you coming back?" I'd only been *gone* two days.

MUNRO. Uh-huh.

WILTEN. I said, "Come on, honey, haven't you ever heard of a bender?" Or she *says* I said, I don't remember. But I mean, back off. Stop suffocating me. I mean — long weekend, right?

MUNRO. Uh-huh.

WILTEN. I got a high-pressure job, I don't need that crap at home. *(Brad squeezes past Wilten through the door and lays a sheet on*

Munro's desk.)

BRAD. Ensiled grains. *(He squeezes past Wilten back out the door.)*

WILTEN. So I'm thinking about separating. You know, cut my losses.

MUNRO. *(Absently, as he leans forward to peer at the sheet.)* Uh-huh … Holy cow. Someone should do something about this. *(He drops the page in the wastebasket and leans back again.)*

WILTEN. But then again, you know, you wake up in some motel room with a strange woman, empty gin bottle, bruises all over your face, *no* idea what's happened — it's nice to have a home to go back to.

MUNRO. Yeah, I hear ya. But maybe you should find a more congenial mate, where you're not always — I mean you've been talking about divorcing Marci for three years now.

WILTEN. Yeah.

MUNRO. You need a stable home life.

WILTEN. Oh, right!

MUNRO. What.

WILTEN. Coming from you?!

MUNRO. What.

WILTEN. Your daughter hates you, correct me if I'm wrong.

MUNRO. Uh-huh.

WILTEN. Your wife doesn't exactly seem crazy about you.

MUNRO. Uh-huh.

WILTEN. And you're talking to me about a stable home life.

MUNRO. Wilten, how long've you known me.

WILTEN. Well — what, six years.

MUNRO. How long have I had these problems?

WILTEN. Six years.

MUNRO. And what does "stable" mean?

WILTEN. Well, okay, yes, in that sense you have a stable home life —

MUNRO. "In that sense"? How many senses does "stable" have? You haven't seen my briefcase, have you?

WILTEN. Well then I didn't mean stable, I meant nurturing.

MUNRO. You didn't *say* stable. *I* said stable.

WILTEN. Well then *you* meant nurturing. No I haven't seen your briefcase.

MUNRO. Don't tell me what I meant. I thought I left it here. But you haven't seen it?

WILTEN. Stable, nurturing, whatever, don't lecture me about —
MUNRO. I? Lecture? No. Lecture? I'll *weigh in*, maybe. Probe, assess; if it's called for I'll remonstrate, yes, but —
WILTEN. Lecture, remonstrate, whatever — the damn semantics are so important to you.
MUNRO. Well words are important. Without words we're just, we're just … what's the word? I thought I brought my briefcase home yesterday but then I couldn't picture myself doing it, so maybe I just left it here. Ever do that? See if you can picture yourself doing something?
WILTEN. Well sure. Something — sexual? *(The phone-intercom buzzes.)*
MUNRO. In a meeting!
WILTEN. Wait. That could have been lunch.

Scene 4

Home.

Munro is on the couch reading the newspaper.

Bobby enters.

MUNRO. Oh — Bobby. You haven't seen my briefcase, have you?
BOBBY. The brown one?
MUNRO. I only have one briefcase.
BOBBY. So, yes, the brown one? *(Munro stares at him.)*
MUNRO. Where do you get that?
BOBBY. Get what. *(Munro stares at him.)*
MUNRO. Bobby, have you seen my brown briefcase?
BOBBY. Why?
MUNRO. Why? Why? Because it's mine. Because I can't find it. Because I need it. Because it's mine.
BOBBY. I see it all the time, Dad. You bring it home every day.
MUNRO. Did you see it yesterday?
BOBBY. Did you bring it home yesterday?

MUNRO. I can't remember. That's why I ask.

BOBBY. I don't know. If something happens all the time you stop seeing it. Can you sign something for school? *(Munro takes the sheet and automatically takes out a pen, but hesitates, looking at it.)*

MUNRO. What is it?

BOBBY. It's you giving permission for me to take Sex Ed. *(Munro stares at the paper, wary of a trap.)*

MUNRO. Ask Mother to sign it.

BOBBY. She said ask you to sign it. *(Munro hesitates.)*

MUNRO. In a negative way or just, get Father to sign it?

BOBBY. Come on, Dad, do you want me to think sex is dirty?

MUNRO. *I* thought sex was dirty. When I was a kid. I still do. And yet here *you* are.

BOBBY. Oh look, Dad, the signature isn't even mandatory. They only gave us these things to promote discussion of the issues at home. *(Munro looks at Bobby, then hastily scribbles his signature.)*

MUNRO. Listen, son. The reason I ask about this briefcase, and why I want you to think about it hard: it had important things in it. From work. If somebody bad, an evildoer, found these important things, and people learned that they came from me, well — Daddy could spend a very very long time in jail.

BOBBY. But it would probably be one of those country club jails, right? *(Munro stares at Bobby.)*

MUNRO. Possibly. Possibly.

Scene 5

Later.

Munro still holds open the newspaper, reading.

He starts to lower it, but something catches his eye and he raises it again. He reads for another long beat, he lowers the paper, folds it, sets it aside and stares brooding at a point in space.

Judy enters.

JUDY. You're not watching the ballgame?
MUNRO. (*Still staring off.*) What's the point.
JUDY. Who do you want to ask on Friday?
MUNRO. (*Absent.*) Ask what.
JUDY. Here. Dinner. Ask here.
MUNRO. Didn't you? Ask someone?
JUDY. Davia and the Littlejohns. You said you might ask someone else. So you'd have someone to talk to.
MUNRO. Nah, that's okay. I don't have to talk.
JUDY. No. People think that's hostile. And weird. Sitting in silence.
MUNRO. People are pests. They should sit more in silence.
JUDY. Bob —
MUNRO. Okay, fine, Wilten and Marci.
JUDY. Wilten and Marci.
MUNRO. Yeah.
JUDY. They throw plates and scream.
MUNRO. They don't literally throw plates.
JUDY. They scream. They pound the table. They discuss their sex lives and make people uncomfortable.
MUNRO. People should be more tolerant. We're not so different. One person from another.
JUDY. Okay. But we're a *little* different. And we *could* ask someone with more to offer than not literally throwing plates. We could aim high. (*Munro broods, gazing off. At length:*)

32

MUNRO. Y'ever think about Bobby? *(Beat.)*

JUDY. Our son? *(Beat.)*

MUNRO. Yeah. *(Another beat. Munro sighs, shakes his head.)* I don't know. I think he should stop watching *SpongeBob*.

JUDY. You've been sitting here figuring that out?

MUNRO. It's his attitude. His worldview. His *weltgeist*. You know what *weltgeist* is.

JUDY. Worldview.

MUNRO. That's ex*act*ly what it is, it's his worldview.

JUDY. Which you think he gets from *SpongeBob*.

MUNRO. It contributes. Don't sneer at me.

JUDY. Okay.

MUNRO. What do you think?

JUDY. He hasn't watched *SpongeBob* in two years.

MUNRO. *(This wakes him.)* Really?

JUDY. He doesn't watch TV much at all now.

MUNRO. *(Genuine curiosity.)* What does he do?

JUDY. Our son?

MUNRO. Yeah.

JUDY. Goes on the internet.

MUNRO. The internet!

JUDY. All the time.

MUNRO. Well the internet is completely unfiltered!

JUDY. Yes.

MUNRO. It's just a massive, swollen, deep river of crud! It's, it's — I'm not even talking about pornography — it's a torrent of idiocy and half-baked ideas and the protocols of the elders of Zion and so forth. I mean anyone can put his moronic ideas on that thing and try to enlist people in his personal insanity. Bobby might just as well go down to the Delaware River and wade in with his mouth open and let the river flow right through him and on out his butthole with all the garbage and disease and grotesque bacteria clinging to his insides where they'll rot and fester and infect his whole body, he might as well do *that!* *(Judy shrugs.)*

JUDY. Okay. Tell him he can't go on the internet. *(Munro stares at her for a beat.)*

MUNRO. Ah, it probably won't hurt him. *(Beat.)*

JUDY. So who are you asking? *(Staring beat.)*

MUNRO. What are the choices?

Scene 6

Office.

Brad stands before Munro's desk, hands thrust into pockets.

BRAD. He says it's worrisome.

MUNRO. Worrisome.

BRAD. Uh-huh.

MUNRO. Well sure it's worrisome. What, here, in this department, we're not gonna worry?

BRAD. No. I mean yes. I mean no.

MUNRO. *Yes* we're gonna worry. That's what we do. We worry. So that other people don't have to. They can if they want but they don't have to. But the point is — you know what the point is?

BRAD. Um —

MUNRO. The point is, we will prevail. Armed only with logic, we can prevail over any animal. Even over our enemy, with all his cruel cunning.

BRAD. And logic. *(Beat.)*

MUNRO. *What.*

BRAD. Cruel cunning and logic. He has logic, too, right? Are you claiming we have a monopoly on logic?

MUNRO. Well ... no ...

BRAD. Are you saying we're the only —

MUNRO. Armed with logic and our way of life. Logic embedded in our national fabric. Which gives us the advantage.

BRAD. Okay.

MUNRO. Okay?

BRAD. Okay.

MUNRO. Not the logic hanging out there all by itself — I mean, Jesus. *(Beat.)*

BRAD. Is that what I should tell him?

MUNRO. Who.

BRAD. Carmody. About the waste site.

MUNRO. Well —

BRAD. I think he wanted a specific recommendation.

MUNRO. *(Nettled.) I* know that! I *know* that! Tell him I'll get back to him! Rome wasn't built in a day! *(Brad turns to go. Munro calms.)*

MUNRO. What are you doing for dinner Friday? *(The question stops Brad at the door.)*

BRAD. What do you mean?

MUNRO. What do I mean? Am I speaking Greek? Or one of the more obscure languages of the Finno-Ugric family? Dinner, Friday. I'm reaching out.

BRAD. Well, I have a, uh …

MUNRO. Fine, forget it. You don't have to stand there stammering.

BRAD. It's just, uh, we've never done anything socially.

MUNRO. Yeah. That's right. And why start. You don't want to come over to my house and chat with a bunch of strangers about your home life.

BRAD. I don't have a home life. I'm not married.

MUNRO. Well, nevertheless —

BRAD. People don't ask bachelors "how's your home life." They ask "how's your sex life."

MUNRO. Well I don't want to know that.

BRAD. No. Yeah. Of course not. *(Hesitates at the door.)* So I'm *not* invited? *(Munro stares at him.)*

MUNRO. No! Why would I want *you* to come over! Forget it, go to hell! *(Brad turns again to go. Munro grimaces.)* Sorry man, I'm sorry. I'm all irritable. I'm worried about my damn briefcase.

BRAD. I'm sorry.

MUNRO. No, *I'm* sorry. It's on me. I'm anxious. And I don't even know if anything's wrong. Everything's fine, for all I know. But I *don't* know. So *I'm* not fine. *(Beat; he looks at Brad as if just noticing him.)* Do you ever feel … right?

BRAD. *(Considers; decides to open up.)* Well … there's a lake I go to … in Canada … *(Munro's look at Brad holds, and curdles, giving Brad to understand that Munro finds this self-revelation not only unhelpful but witless. Seeking to escape eye contact, Brad finds a friend in the face of his watch.)* I, uh … *(Jerks a thumb over his shoulder.)* Anthrax meeting. *(He hastily withdraws. Munro's look stays on Brad until he is safely out the door. Then a weary head shake, and he leans forward to hit a button on the phone.)*

MUNRO. Is lunch here?

SECRETARY. You didn't order any, sir.

MUNRO. *(Testy.)* So no, it's not here. *(Rises.)* Going out then.

Scene 7

Office. Empty. A brown briefcase sits on Munro's desk.

The noise of scraping in the lock. The lock turns. The knob turns. The door opens.

Munro enters, overcoated. He trudges, downcast, to a closet, opens it, shucks the overcoat, hangs it.

He turns toward his desk and comes up short, staring at the briefcase. A beat.

He turns again to face the closet, his back to the desk. For a long beat he faces the closet door.

He whirls to take the briefcase unawares.

It is still there.

He approaches it cautiously. He inspects it, runs his hands over it. He squeezes the clasp to release its tongue. He opens it. He leafs through the papers inside without withdrawing them. He half pulls out an old sweater for a better view in.

Satisfied, he restuffs the sweater and snaps down the tongue. He hoists the briefcase and walks back and forth holding it, smiling, feeling the familiar weight.

He sets it back down on the desktop. He hits a button on the phone.

MUNRO. Dolores?

SECRETARY. Yes sir.

MUNRO. Who came into my office during lunch?

SECRETARY. No one, sir. *(Beat.)*

MUNRO. Were you?

SECRETARY. ... Sir?

MUNRO. In my office?

SECRETARY. Sir, I'm not allowed a key.

MUNRO. That's right. You're goddamn right you're not. *(Beat.)* Thank you, Dolores. *(He looks slowly around the office, thinking. His look settles on the two office windows. He goes to the windows. He pushes up on one. It will not slide: locked. He pushes up on the other. It slides open. He ducks and leans out. He looks along the ledge one way. He looks along the ledge the other way. He looks down. He draws back in, thinking. He leans out again. He looks up. His look catches on something. He leans further out, body twisting, to get a view up the building. His neck cranes. Something interests him. His grip, curled around the bottom of the window, slips. His weight carries him out, legs sliding over the sill, and he screams, dropping. His scream recedes.)*

Scene 8

Home.

An investigator in a suit, holding a small spiral notebook, has a chair pulled up to face Judy who sits on the couch, a handkerchief laced through the fingers of one hand.

A long beat.

JUDY. Not really.

INVESTIGATOR. Despondent?

JUDY. No.

INVESTIGATOR. Agitated?

JUDY. No.

INVESTIGATOR. Short?

JUDY. Short — testy? No.

INVESTIGATOR. Did he —

JUDY. Not more than usual.

INVESTIGATOR. Did he have money worries? That you knew of?

JUDY. No. No no. He was worried about his briefcase.

INVESTIGATOR. Why?

JUDY. He'd ... mislaid it. I think.

INVESTIGATOR. Why do you think that?

JUDY. Because he said he'd mislaid it. *(Beat.)* He was worried he'd go to jail.

INVESTIGATOR. For mislaying his briefcase?

JUDY. Or disciplined. Or I don't know.

INVESTIGATOR. Mm.

JUDY. That it would be a black mark. A blotch. I mean a blot.

INVESTIGATOR. So you think that might have ... led to ...

JUDY. No no. No no.

INVESTIGATOR. Uh-huh.

JUDY. Not that worried.

INVESTIGATOR. Okay. *(Beat.)* Do *you* have any theories?

JUDY. I guess — maybe — he felt things more deeply than I knew.

INVESTIGATOR. And he had deep feelings about ... ?

JUDY. *(Nodding)* Nothing I knew of.

INVESTIGATOR. Uh-huh. *(He thumbs back through his notebook, considering his notes.)* Uh-huh. Okay. *(He flips the notebook shut and stands.)* Thank you. *(Beat.)*

JUDY. That's it?

INVESTIGATOR. Uh-huh.

JUDY. The whole investigation?

INVESTIGATOR. Yes.

JUDY. But — but — didn't he know top-secret things?

INVESTIGATOR. Some. *(Chuckles.)* "Some." Duh. He didn't know *all* the top-secret things. *(A beat.)*

JUDY. So — you don't have concerns? About top-secret hanky-panky? Or ... entanglements? Involvements? His briefcase, um, that things, that this thing might, some secret, one thing leading to another — leading to his briefcase —

INVESTIGATOR. Well sure. Sure we have concerns.

JUDY. But you're giving up. Closing the investigation.

INVESTIGATOR. You think if I hang around asking more questions I'll figure this thing out? We can't figure out everything, ma'am. Bad people want to destroy our way of life. They'd love it if I sat here obsessing about this.

JUDY. But you're supposed to chase down everything! You're the bulwark!

INVESTIGATOR. *Bulwark!* Ma'am, with respect, don't be naïve. Yes, we try to anticipate all the bad things that could happen. And then what. What. Vice president of the United States shoots somebody in the face. Ouch. Didn't see that coming. Bad. Bad for the guy who got shot in the face. Bad for everyone. Why? Why because we lose our bearings. Thought we'd identified the threat. Staked out the field of battle. We're set. Ready to respond. And then whoa, vice president starts shooting people in the face. Hadn't thought of that one. Throws us off balance. Gotta recalibrate; pictured the world a certain way, it wasn't quite right. Anticipate *every*thing? Explain *every*thing? (Amounts to the same thing: show how this or that *could* have been anticipated.) That's our job. Yet — can't be done. Yet — that's our job. Okay. Fine. But it can't be done. Especially since it's a human game, human players, mysteries of the heart. Why did your husband kill himself? What was he thinking? feeling? dreading? Beats me. *(He clicks shut his ballpoint pen.)* Move on. *(He looks around. He looks back at Judy, hesitates. Voice lowered:)* Do you have a toilet?

Scene 9

Home, later.

Little Bobby is typing at a computer keyboard. The clack of his typing rattles through the dialog with occasional pauses when he stops to read the screen.

Wilten is seated on the couch next to Judy.

WILTEN. Raisins, of course. Walnuts. Oil and vinegar, believe it or not. And *we* put in a little lemon. *(A cling-wrapped casserole dish on the table may be the object of discussion.)*

JUDY. It's very thoughtful. Thank you.

WILTEN. Oh, look.

JUDY. Very thoughtful. And thank Marci for me.

WILTEN. Oh, no, look. Just carrot salad. *(Beat.)*

JUDY. How *is* Marci?

WILTEN. She's a pain in the ass. *(It slipped out; he recovers.)* She's fine. She's good. *(Beat.)*

JUDY. People have been very kind.

WILTEN. Well of course they have. How could they not. Given what, um … Bob was such a … Well, you know what Bob was. And you. You're … so strong, and a very … handsome woman.

JUDY. *(After an alarmed beat she deflects, looking at Bobby.)* Unbelievable, how he does that all day. At his age.

WILTEN. Oh, yeah. Internet. I mean you should see at the office. There used to be a social thing at work. You could drop by someone's desk, just chew the rag. Can't talk to anyone anymore. I mean you can but they're typing while they talk. One eye on you one eye on the screen. If that. I don't think it's good. Well of course it's good. Great tool. But you can't say it's all good.

JUDY. No no — swollen crud.

WILTEN. Excuse me?

JUDY. What're you doing there, Bobby? *(Bobby types on.)* Bobby? *(He pauses.)*

BOBBY. *(Fiercely, as he peers at the screen.)* I'm gonna find out what happened to Dad. *(Another beat reading the screen. He resumes typing.)*

End of Play

STRUGGLE SESSION

CHARACTERS

BUM

COLLEAGUE

SECOND COLLEAGUE

THIRD COLLEAGUE

LURY

BECK

SCHILLING

STRUGGLE SESSION

Scene 1

An office. Two men.

SCHILLING. And then during the summer round-ups your team overstated the net by at least 20%.
BECK. Uh-huh.
SCHILLING. And you know what kind of disadvantage that puts us in, when we try to plan the next quarter.
BECK. Uh-huh.
SCHILLING. I mean this is serious shit.
BECK. Sure.
SCHILLING. It's thumb-up-our-ass time. Wiggling. It's Hello, we're fucked.
BECK. You know it was Koski's figures we were relying on.
SCHILLING. No I don't know that.
BECK. Okay well I'm telling you.
SCHILLING. Okay well I know *that*, but I'm saying it doesn't matter.
BECK. Doesn't matter whose figures it is? Whose fault it is?
SCHILLING. It's *your* fault. You rely on his figures that's *your* decision. You gotta know it's right, man.
BECK. How am I gonna know.
SCHILLING. You gotta know it's right. Or not.
BECK. Well how am I gonna know.
SCHILLING. In whatever fashion. You gotta know. And that's not why you're fired anyway.
BECK. Okay.
SCHILLING. Okay?
BECK. Okay, so why am I fired? *(Beat.)*
SCHILLING. I just explained.

43

BECK. You explained why I *wasn't* being fired.
SCHILLING. No, I —
BECK. The summer round-ups.
SCHILLING. No.
BECK. Is *not* why.
SCHILLING. Yes.
BECK. *Are* not. You said. Why.
SCHILLING. Uh-huh.
BECK. So why. Why am I being fired. *(Staring beat.)*
SCHILLING. It's the pattern. *(Beat.)*
BECK. The pattern.
SCHILLING. Uh-huh.
BECK. Of what.
SCHILLING. The pattern of fucking up.
BECK. The pattern of *my* fucking up?
SCHILLING. I'm gonna fire you for the pattern of someone else's fucking up? Okay, what, waitaminute, we're debating? Whether or not you're fired? No. I don't think so. I think I'm *telling* you you're fired.
BECK. Uh-huh.
SCHILLING. I mean like it's like, "You're fired." That's what I'm saying.
BECK. Aren't I entitled to know why? Because, wouldn't most people say, okay, outline, A, B, C, this is why you're fired?
SCHILLING. Most people aren't running this department. *I* am running this department. And guess what. I answer to Elements just like you answer to me, and we're not, like, dismantling all that because one guy, one guy, you, doesn't happen to like being fired.
BECK. Uh-huh.
SCHILLING. This is bigger than that.
BECK. Okay.
SCHILLING. And you have blinkers on. "Why am I fired? Why am I fired?" Maybe *you* don't understand, but I have to answer to Elements. If you can understand *that.* And I guess you can't, and, um, so be it.
BECK. I understand the heirarchy. That there's a heirarchy.
SCHILLING. You're goddamn right there is.
BECK. But that doesn't tell me how I fucked up.
SCHILLING. Well I think my vision here is broader than yours.
BECK. Okay. Maybe, maybe not.

SCHILLING. It's not a maybe, okay.
BECK. Uh-huh.
SCHILLING. It's a definite, like, "You're fired." Not a maybe.
BECK. I understand that.
SCHILLING. Well, whether you do or not. You're fired.

Scene 2

Another office. Two men: Schilling, firer from the previous scene; and Lury, older.

LURY. Uh-huh.
SCHILLING. Just constant bitching.
LURY. Uh-huh.
SCHILLING. Constant, constant bitching. And constant, you know, demands that you justify, whatever, explain, whatever.
LURY. Right.
SCHILLING. Blah blah blah.
LURY. Boy.
SCHILLING. The sense of entitlement. Amazing.
LURY. Uh-huh.
SCHILLING. Anyway.
LURY. Yeah. Well, thanks for coming in, John.
SCHILLING. Uh-huh.
LURY. John, um … we're not happy with the way things are going.
SCHILLING. *(Suddenly uneasy.)* What?
LURY. Morale is not good in your department.
SCHILLING. Mo*rale.*
LURY. And the work suffers accordingly.
SCHILLING. And that's *my* fault?!
LURY. Talking to your people, generally, we get back a consistent, um, unhappiness. They complain about decisions made they don't understand, arbitrary firings, et cetera. They —
SCHILLING. Well, you want to find disgruntled assholes, go look in *any* department!

LURY. Sure. But I don't think we have a steady hand on the helm here.

SCHILLING. Steady *hand!*

LURY. In your department, I don't think we have a steady hand. That's certainly the perception. And I think it's the reality. And so we're letting you go.

SCHILLING. What the fuck! *What?!*

Scene 3

A street corner. A bum sits leaning against a wall, a paper cup for change in front of him.

Schilling passes by.

BUM. Got a quarter? *(Schilling stops. He stares at the bum for a beat.)*

SCHILLING. I got fired today. *(Beat.)*

BUM. A dime?

SCHILLING. Have you ever been fired?

BUM. This isn't about me.

SCHILLING. Have you ever had a goddamn fucking job?

BUM. Yeah I've had jobs. Shit jobs. Never had a suit job. You're lucky.

SCHILLING. Yeah, right.

BUM. Here. You sit here. Bitch baby. I'll give you my cup, you give me your suit. And your, you know, whatever it is you use to get those jobs.

SCHILLING. How about I stick your Dixie cup up your fucking butthole.

BUM. How about you don't, jackass.

SCHILLING. I *worked* to where I could get those jobs, asshole. It's called accomplishment. It's not some little rabbit's foot I —

BUM. Yeah yeah.

SCHILLING. — carry around in my fucking pocket that got me the job. Here, give me an enormous amount of responsibility, see I got a little rabbit's foot. Dumbfuck.

BUM. Oh, like I couldn't do your job? Aren't *you* the cucumber in the gardener's ass!

SCHILLING. How about I kick you till you bleed out of every hole in your fucking body. Blood and snot coming out of you everywhere.

BUM. Power-tripper.

SCHILLING. Fuckhead. Fucker. Piece of shit fuck.

Scene 4

Same corner, same bum, later.

Beck passes by.

BUM. Got a quarter? *(Beck stops and stares at the bum.)*

BECK. I got fired today. *(Beat.)*

BUM. Did *I* fire you? *(Beck hesitates. Rather than get into it, he drops a quarter into the cup.)* God bless you. Another guy came by an hour ago, said *he'd* been fired. No quarter, busting my balls.

BECK. Well, you'd lash out, too.

BUM. Ah, he was a fuck. I used to be in the merchant marine. I worked harder than that gazool ever worked in his whole fucking life, made my living by the sweat of my brow. I don't give a shit about his shit.

BECK. His shit is a big deal to him.

BUM. He's still in the suit. I'm in the fucking this.

BECK. He doesn't care about his suit. He's used to the suit. You get used to what you've got. You know, the floor drops out, if it's a higher floor it's even worse. You go whoa, shit.

BUM. Don't give me sympathy and understanding. The guy was a jackass.

BECK. Well just don't act all superior just because you're a bum.

BUM. Yeah yeah.

BECK. That crap might impress some people.

BUM. Fuck you.

BECK. I gotta go home, tell my wife I got fired. Try not to feel like a loser.

BUM. Oh wow. I wouldn't know how *that* feels. *(Beck sits next to the bum, starting to engage.)*

BECK. What do you do? How do you deal with it?

BUM. Deal with...?

BECK. Disappointment. Bumness.

BUM. You gotta go beyond it. You accept those terms, you *are* a loser. You gotta use different terms.

BECK. Yeah. Okay. Like wife, she loves me, there's love.

BUM. *I* can't use that one. *(Beat.)* Or roof over my head, or any of that shit.

BECK. Uh-huh.

BUM. My terms are more, it isn't raining. Or else, there's an eave. *(Beat.)* You improvise.

BECK. Uh-huh.

BUM. Attainable shit. Philosophers and so forth have said this and it's true. I mean it doesn't speak to worth, maybe. Personal worth. But those are the terms we're rejecting. Life is a journey, not a race. Got a quarter? *(This is directed at Lury, passing. He stops and digs in his pocket.)* God bless you.

LURY. Don't I know you?

BUM. Were you in the merchant marine?

LURY. No, *you*. Aren't you in John Schilling's department?

BECK. He fired me today.

LURY. Really.

BECK. Mm.

LURY. So you're apprenticing here?

BUM. Funny.

LURY. I'm Arthur Lury. Elements. Why don't you come back.

BECK. Come back. What'll Schilling say?

LURY. He's gone.

BUM. Don't do it.

BECK. Gone?

LURY. Fired. I'm offering you his job.

BUM. Don't do it. Big mistake.

BECK. *(To Lury.)* Really?

LURY. Really.

BECK. Huh. *(A thought.)* If you hire me to be Schilling, who replaces me?

LURY. Whoever you hire. You're him now. You decide.

BECK. Really? Up to me?

LURY. Sure. Just make it work.

BECK. I run the department. Hire who I want.

LURY. Just make it work.

BUM. Yeah. Which is how it starts.

Scene 5

In black.

BECK. What?! *(Lights come up on Schilling's former office. Beck sits at Schilling's former desk. He stares at a piece of paper, very still, and after a beat repeats a horrified:)* What?! *(He picks up the phone and dials. After a beat:)* Jonathan, I'm looking at these, these L-10's on the winter round-ups and I, I, I just can't believe, I mean this just doesn't add up. I mean this is bullshit. Could you come down here immediately and … Well whose numbers are they? … *My* new guy? … These reflect the numbers he gave you? … No, that's all right, I'll call him … No, it's fine. You're fine. Sorry. I'll call him.

Scene 6

A cubicle.

Its occupant is the bum, now cleaned up and in a suit, but still sporting his luxuriant bum beard. He stands with an arm draped over the left clothboard partition, talking to the man in the neighboring cubicle.

BUM. And then I invented this sexual position. Mind-blowing. I mean yes there was discomfort. It made you a little sore. And in unguarded moments, farts. But a hell of a position. Gave enormous pleasure to the broad. *(A quick buzz from the telephone. Both men ignore it. A silent beat.)* Just enormous pleasure to the broad.

COLLEAGUE. What was it?

BUM. What.

COLLEAGUE. What was it?

BUM. What *was* it? *(Two quick buzzes from the telephone. Another beat.)* What was the position?

COLLEAGUE. Yeah.

BUM. I'm gonna tell *you*?

COLLEAGUE. Why not? *(The bum smiles, shaking his head.)*

BUM. No.

COLLEAGUE. Why not?

BUM. First of all, hard to describe. Secondly, I've been burned on this before.

COLLEAGUE. Burned.

BUM. Oh yeah. But I will tell you this. You need your hands free.

COLLEAGUE. Why wouldn't they be free?

BUM. All four hands. *(A long buzz. A beat.)*

COLLEAGUE. The two of you.

BUM. Uh-huh.

COLLEAGUE. Why wouldn't they be free?

BUM. They — huh?

COLLEAGUE. You're having sex, what else would you be doing? Knitting?

BUM. Okay, yeah. Fine. Forget it. *(Three short impatient buzzes.)*

COLLEAGUE. Fine. Forget it. You're bullshitting me. Is that your phone?

BUM. Bullshitting you. Well, let me tell you something, my little lamefucker friend. One of the broads I pleasured in this manner, she was in publishing, very high up, a name you would recognize if I was the type to name names.

COLLEAGUE. I don't know anyone in publishing.

BUM. Nevertheless. So she wants me to write a book about it. The position. Outlining it. Pictures, text. A surefire bestseller, in her estimation. A can't-miss. But then I —

COLLEAGUE. Can gays do it? *(Beat.)*

BUM. Are you gay?

COLLEAGUE. No. *(Beat. The bum clears his throat.)*

BUM. But then I go to this movie. I attend a movie. And someone has obviously spilt the beanerinos.

COLLEAGUE. Because there it is.

BUM. Uh-huh.

COLLEAGUE. In all its glory.

BUM. Roger. *(Beat.)*

COLLEAGUE. What kind of movie? *(Beat.)*

BUM. Not mainstream.

COLLEAGUE. Did she know someone in the movie? Or working on it? Like on the crew?

BUM. Who?

COLLEAGUE. The publishing chick.

BUM. Well yes, clearly. Did you understand what I said?

COLLEAGUE. Yes.

BUM. Exact same position?

COLLEAGUE. Yeah, but can you rule out that, independently, two people, or more, even, maybe, could, could devise —

BUM. Oh come on. *(A very, very long buzz. Another beat.)*

COLLEAGUE. Does it have to do with the ass? *(Beat.)* Or anus? *(Considering beat.)*

BUM. Anus proper?

Scene 7

The bum is now at the water cooler, arm draped over it.

BUM. You've seen ventriloquists? Who can drink from a glass of water and while they drink the dummy keeps talking? Sexually, this is the equivalent.

SECOND COLLEAGUE. Uh-huh. And you —

BUM. Yeah. I devised it.

SECOND COLLEAGUE. Uh-huh.

BUM. And there's some discomfort, sure.

SECOND COLLEAGUE. Uh-huh.

BUM. But it gives enormous pleasure to the broad.

SECOND COLLEAGUE. Uh-huh.

BUM. So, you know. *(Beat.)*

SECOND COLLEAGUE. I don't get it.

BUM. What.

SECOND COLLEAGUE. A to B.

BUM. What.

SECOND COLLEAGUE. How that got you here.

BUM. Well.

SECOND COLLEAGUE. You said long story, long story, and then —

BUM. Yeah, right. Well. So like I said, there's some soreness. And I'm visiting my ladyfriend's place. And as I'm going in this guy is leaving the building, walking, a little, like, you know. And I think, Uh-huh. Okay. Because the discomfort is pretty distinctive. I think, is this broad, is she, has she taken it upon herself to school some other, I mean it seems this fuckstance of mine is no longer *entre nous*.

SECOND COLLEAGUE. Yeah.

BUM. It's a very telltale, I know exactly how you cramp up. Stretching that way. And then there are some other things, a mutual friend of ours, I start to notice, he's favoring his, he's also sort of, you know, walking in this telltale fashion.

SECOND COLLEAGUE. Right.

BUM. I mean, it's like, eventually you wouldn't believe the number of people in the neighborhood. Walking around like that. And I'm thinking, what is *with* this broad.

SECOND COLLEAGUE. Uh-huh.

BUM. And then I start seeing it in movies, fucking *movies*, I was a movie buff for a while there. And I think, all right this is a slut. I'm outta here. And I join the merchant marine.

SECOND COLLEAGUE. Okay.

BUM. Right, which is fine for a while but then there's a problem with my seaman's papers. Not being current. Allegedly. According to the business agent. Who is a fucking asshole. Not that — nothing against Jews in general. But anyway, I'm out on the street.

SECOND COLLEAGUE. And you meet Beck.

BUM. Great guy.

SECOND COLLEAGUE. Panhandling.

BUM. Yeah. And he gets hired back —

SECOND COLLEAGUE. Schilling's job.

BUM. — yeah, and he hires me. *(Beat.)*

SECOND COLLEAGUE. Can you, like, is there a patent? Or something? That you could take out? On the position?

BUM. Well now you're talking lawyers and shit and a whole world of —
SECOND COLLEAGUE. Right.
BUM. — of fucking and getting fucked. Which I am not into.
SECOND COLLEAGUE. Right. Right right right.
BUM. Not enough money in the world.
SECOND COLLEAGUE. Right. I hear ya.
BUM. And, which, I don't know, maybe this should belong to the public anyway.
SECOND COLLEAGUE. Uh-huh.
BUM. I mean do I wanna be Bill Gates.

Scene 8

The bum is back in his cubicle, arm now draped over the right partition wall, talking to his other neighbor.

BUM. Sort of like, you know, rubbing circles on your stomach while you pat your other hand up and down on your head?
THIRD COLLEAGUE. Uh-huh.
BUM. Not everyone can do it. *(Beat.)* Gives enormous pleasure to the broad. *(A very long and then a short buzz from the telephone.)* For fuck's sake. *(Picks up phone and barks:)* Hello!

Scene 9

Beck's office.

The bum and Beck. A still beat. Finally:

BECK. I don't know.
BUM. Only one. But the lightbulb has got to *want* to change.

(Beat.) Get it?

BECK. I'm gonna have to let you go. *(Beat.)*

BUM. Let me go what.

BECK. ... Let you —

BUM. Let me go scratch my balls?

BECK. You know, let you go. Let you ... I'm gonna have to ... You're fired.

BUM. Fired.

BECK. Fired. Yes.

BUM. Like, you're fired.

BECK. Well. *(Beat.)* If that's the way you wanna put it.

BUM. So you're the company man now.

BECK. I'm sorry.

BUM. Right. I see.

BECK. They gave me this job expecting that I would work, and, you know, make sure other people did their work. That's part of my job.

BUM. Company fucking man.

BECK. Hey, come on, man! You don't want to do the company work, don't take the company fucking pay, man! *(Back to penitent.)* I'm sorry.

BUM. Who says I haven't been doing the work!

BECK. Oh come on, man!

BUM. Who says!

BECK. You sit around bullshitting! You ass around!

BUM. You call it bullshit! I'll tell you what's bullshit.

BECK. Yeah, okay!

BUM. You expect me to climb the corporate ladder. Apply myself. So that — what? So that some day *I* can fire people? Make *them* feel shitty? You said the job would be fun. *Fun.* That's what I signed on for. Not power trips.

BECK. Look, I, I'm not a bad person.

BUM. You're a fucking saint. They should build a fucking temple to you, man. Light candles.

BECK. Whatever.

BUM. Rows and rows of flickering candles.

BECK. Whatever.

BUM. Scented. Like angel farts.

BECK. I'm just doing what I'm supposed to do.

BUM. You're just ass-climbing. Climbing the ass of man.

BECK. No way.

BUM. I tried to educate you. Plant the seed. But the ground was barren, clearly. And where the ground is barren jackshit'll sprout.

BECK. I am not climbing the ass of man. *(Beat.)* I'm sorry.

BUM. You're sorry? It's okay. For me it was just an experiment. *(Heads to door.)* I still got a street corner to go back to. And a soul. I'm sorry for *you*, man. *(He leaves. A long beat. Beck sits with his head in his hands. He swings the phone around and dials. After a beat:)*

BECK. Honey, something bad just happened — *I'm* fine, but, um, I just had to tell a guy he was fired — not just *tell* him he was fired, I was the one that fired him. Making me the firer. So that now, on account of me, there's a guy walking around, fired. Now: does that make me an asshole? A firing asshole? Climbing the ass of man? Or not? *Not* necessarily? Not in every universe? Okay. Um … Hope your day is going well. *(He hangs up. He sighs. He stares. He holds down a talk button on the phone console.)* Dorothy, if my wife calls put her through. *(He releases the button and eases back. He hastily leans forward again for the talk button.)* Like you always do. I'm not saying you wouldn't. No criticism. But if my wife calls, um … put her through. *(He releases the button. He props head in hands and stares at the phone. He waits.)*

Scene 10

The street corner, the bum back at his post. He is still in his suit but it is now frayed and soiled and his hair has reverted to tangles.

BUM. Got a quarter? *(A pedestrian — he has long locks and a mustache and wears a beaded headband and a fringed vest and other accoutrements of a free spirit — drops a quarter in the bum's paper cup.)*

PEDESTRIAN. Hey, man.

BUM. God bless you. *(The pedestrian lingers — insisting, after a beat:)*

PEDESTRIAN. Hey, man. *(The bum takes in the man's attire. He waves the two-fingered peace sign.)*

BUM. Peace.

PEDESTRIAN. Don't you remember me? *(Staring beat.)*

BUM. Were you in the merchant marine?

PEDESTRIAN. I had short hair, came by here a few months ago, I was all uptight, gave you a hard time 'cause I'd just been fired.

BUM. Yeah. Yeah yeah. You were the first guy.

PEDESTRIAN. *(Schilling.)* Huh?

BUM. Long story.

SCHILLING. I was hoping you'd still be here. See, before I drop out, I'm going around and apologizing to everyone I was an asshole to.

BUM. Wow.

SCHILLING. Lotta stops.

BUM. Uh-huh.

SCHILLING. Trying to chop off that karma, man. Don't wanna drag it with me.

BUM. You've changed.

SCHILLING. Yeah. Getting fired really shook me up. Yanked the rug out. I dropped, man. 'Til I hit bottom. Woke up in the gutter one day, pants clammy with my own piss, and I began — well, I *hope* it was my piss — I began to think, man, maybe I shouldn't have bought into that whole winner/loser thing society tries to sell you.

BUM. Right.

SCHILLING. So I pulled myself together and delt a little dope.

BUM. Uh-huh.

SCHILLING. Made enough money to buy a VW bus. Now me and my new lady are gonna paint it day-glo and hit the road and get a groove on, fuck like crazy and have lots of kids and raise 'em barefoot on the bus.

BUM. Right on.

SCHILLING. So, I'm sorry I was an asshole.

BUM. Oh, that's okay. You got the right idea. Squeeze the lessons from the past, then throw it away. Don't pack it. I envy you. You found a good lady?

SCHILLING. Oh man. She is unbelievable. In touch with the spiritual. In touch with the physical. Makes love like a bobcat on a rocking chair. Taught *me* a thing or two.

BUM. That's great.

SCHILLING. Yeah.

BUM. And she's down with dropping out? What was her bag?

SCHILLING. Publishing. *(Beat.)* You been good? Been here this whole time?

BUM. Nah. Tried the corporate thing for a while.

SCHILLING. Oh yeah?

BUM. It was bullshit.

SCHILLING. Yeah.

BUM. The past is dead. Life is beautiful — if you let it be. Noam Chomsky has explained this.

SCHILLING. Uh-huh. Well, peace, man.

BUM. Peace. *(Schilling leaves, exhibiting a mild limp. The bum watches him go. He calls out with an afterthought though Schilling has disappeared:)* Peace *and* love! *(No answer from the wings. The bum looks idly into his cup, shakes it, jingling the coins.)* Peace *and* love.

Scene 11

Original office. Beck behind his desk, Lury perched on it.

After a long beat:

LURY. That's it. That's all. Just wanted to say it.

BECK. Okay. Well. Thanks.

LURY. Thank *you.* There's a good feeling out there. People feel good. Appreciated. Their work shows it. Your department has really shaped up. You're doing great. You're doing great. *(Beat.)* Are you all right?

BECK. I had to fire someone.

LURY. Oh. I'm sorry. Never pleasant.

BECK. Does that make me an asshole?

LURY. Oh no. I'm sure you had to. Not everyone can cut the mustard. Don't drag it with you. *(Rising to go he clenches an encouraging fist.)* Onward. Onward. Good work. *(Stops short.)* One question.

BECK. Yes?

LURY. Who's the hippie in your waiting room? *(Beat.)*

BECK. Schilling.

LURY. No.

BECK. Uh-huh.

LURY. Didn't recognize him.

BECK. Well.

LURY. What does he want?

BECK. To apologize. Dorothy said.

LURY. Really.

BECK. Uh-huh.

LURY. For what.

BECK. Wouldn't tell her.

LURY. Ah. Only you.

BECK. Uh-huh.

LURY. And you haven't seen him.

BECK. Not yet. Busy.

LURY. How long has he been here? *(Beck looks at his watch for a beat, looks up to answer, stops short, and looks back down at his watch. Another beat.)*

BECK. Five hours. *(Beat.)*

LURY. Why not see him. Let him apologize. Move on.

BECK. Okay. Maybe.

LURY. He can't hurt you now. He's a hippie. *(Answerless beat.)* Well, suit yourself. We each find our own way.

BECK. Yeah. To what? *(Lury pauses, hand on the door he has just opened. He is looking out. A long beat.)*

LURY. Boy. Look at that hair. *(Fade out.)*

End of Play

PROPERTY LIST

PEER REVIEW
Papers
Small paper cones of water
Cardboard box, desk items
Stapler
Newspapers

HOMELAND SECURITY
Paper, pen
Briefcase with papers, sweater
Notebook, pen
Handkerchief
Casserole dish
Laptop

STRUGGLE SESSION
Paper cup, change

SOUND EFFECTS

HOMELAND SECURITY
Phone buzz

NEW PLAYS

★ **YELLOW FACE by David Henry Hwang.** Asian-American playwright DHH leads a protest against the casting of Jonathan Pryce as the Eurasian pimp in the original Broadway production of *Miss Saigon*, condemning the practice as "yellowface." The lines between truth and fiction blur with hilarious and moving results in this unreliable memoir. "A pungent play of ideas with a big heart." –*Variety.* "Fabulously inventive." –*The New Yorker.* [5M, 2W] ISBN: 978-0-8222-2301-6

★ **33 VARIATIONS by Moisés Kaufmann.** A mother coming to terms with her daughter. A composer coming to terms with his genius. And, even though they're separated by 200 years, these two people share an obsession that might, even just for a moment, make time stand still. "A compellingly original and thoroughly watchable play for today." –*Talkin' Broadway.* [4M, 4W] ISBN: 978-0-8222-2392-4

★ **BOOM by Peter Sinn Nachtrieb.** A grad student's online personal ad lures a mysterious journalism student to his subterranean research lab. But when a major catastrophic event strikes the planet, their date takes on evolutionary significance and the fate of humanity hangs in the balance. "Darkly funny dialogue." –*NY Times.* "Literate, coarse, thoughtful, sweet, scabrously inappropriate." –*Washington City Paper.* [1M, 2W] ISBN: 978-0-8222-2370-2

★ **LOVE, LOSS AND WHAT I WORE by Nora Ephron and Delia Ephron, based on the book by Ilene Beckerman.** A play of monologues and ensemble pieces about women, clothes and memory covering all the important subjects—mothers, prom dresses, mothers, buying bras, mothers, hating purses and why we only wear black. "Funny, compelling." –*NY Times.* "So funny and so powerful." –*WowOwow.com.* [5W] ISBN: 978-0-8222-2355-9

★ **CIRCLE MIRROR TRANSFORMATION by Annie Baker.** When four lost New Englanders enrolled in Marty's community center drama class experiment with harmless games, hearts are quietly torn apart, and tiny wars of epic proportions are waged and won. "Absorbing, unblinking and sharply funny." –*NY Times.* [2M, 3W] ISBN: 978-0-8222-2445-7

★ **BROKE-OLOGY by Nathan Louis Jackson.** The King family has weathered the hardships of life and survived with their love for each other intact. But when two brothers are called home to take care of their father, they find themselves strangely at odds. "Engaging dialogue." –*TheaterMania.com.* "Assured, bighearted." –*Time Out.* [3M, 1W] ISBN: 978-0-8222-2428-0

DRAMATISTS PLAY SERVICE, INC.
440 Park Avenue South, New York, NY 10016 212-683-8960 Fax 212-213-1539
postmaster@dramatists.com   www.dramatists.com

NEW PLAYS

★ **A CIVIL WAR CHRISTMAS: AN AMERICAN MUSICAL CELEBRA-TION by Paula Vogel, music by Daryl Waters.** It's 1864, and Washington, D.C. is settling down to the coldest Christmas Eve in years. Intertwining many lives, this musical shows us that the gladness of one's heart is the best gift of all. "Boldly inventive theater, warm and affecting." *–Talkin' Broadway.* "Crisp strokes of dialogue." *–NY Times.* [12M, 5W] ISBN: 978-0-8222-2361-0

★ **SPEECH & DEBATE by Stephen Karam.** Three teenage misfits in Salem, Oregon discover they are linked by a sex scandal that's rocked their town. "Savvy comedy." *–Variety.* "Hilarious, cliché-free, and immensely entertaining." *–NY Times.* "A strong, rangy play." *–NY Newsday.* [2M, 2W] ISBN: 978-0-8222-2286-6

★ **DIVIDING THE ESTATE by Horton Foote.** Matriarch Stella Gordon is determined not to divide her 100-year-old Texas estate, despite her family's declining wealth and the looming financial crisis. But her three children have another plan. "Goes for laughs and succeeds." *–NY Daily News.* "The theatrical equivalent of a page-turner." *–Bloomberg.com.* [4M, 9W] ISBN: 978-0-8222-2398-6

★ **WHY TORTURE IS WRONG, AND THE PEOPLE WHO LOVE THEM by Christopher Durang.** Christopher Durang turns political humor upside down with this raucous and provocative satire about America's growing homeland "insecurity." "A smashing new play." *–NY Observer.* "You may laugh yourself silly." *–Bloomberg News.* [4M, 3W] ISBN: 978-0-8222-2401-3

★ **FIFTY WORDS by Michael Weller.** While their nine-year-old son is away for the night on his first sleepover, Adam and Jan have an evening alone together, beginning a suspenseful nightlong roller-coaster ride of revelation, rancor, passion and humor. "Mr. Weller is a bold and productive dramatist." *–NY Times.* [1M, 1W] ISBN: 978-0-8222-2348-1

★ **BECKY'S NEW CAR by Steven Dietz.** Becky Foster is caught in middle age, middle management and in a middling marriage—with no prospects for change on the horizon. Then one night a socially inept and grief-struck millionaire stumbles into the car dealership where Becky works. "Gently and consistently funny." *–Variety.* "Perfect blend of hilarious comedy and substantial weight." *–Broadway Hour.* [4M, 3W] ISBN: 978-0-8222-2393-1

DRAMATISTS PLAY SERVICE, INC.
440 Park Avenue South, New York, NY 10016 212-683-8960 Fax 212-213-1539
postmaster@dramatists.com www.dramatists.com

NEW PLAYS

★ **AT HOME AT THE ZOO by Edward Albee.** Edward Albee delves deeper into his play THE ZOO STORY by adding a first act, HOMELIFE, which precedes Peter's fateful meeting with Jerry on a park bench in Central Park. "An essential and heartening experience." *–NY Times.* "Darkly comic and thrilling." *–Time Out.* "Genuinely fascinating." *–Journal News.* [2M, 1W] ISBN: 978-0-8222-2317-7

★ **PASSING STRANGE book and lyrics by Stew, music by Stew and Heidi Rodewald, created in collaboration with Annie Dorsen.** A daring musical about a young bohemian that takes you from black middle-class America to Amsterdam, Berlin and beyond on a journey towards personal and artistic authenticity. "Fresh, exuberant, bracingly inventive, bitingly funny, and full of heart." *–NY Times.* "The freshest musical in town!" *–Wall Street Journal.* "Excellent songs and a vulnerable heart." *–Variety.* [4M, 3W] ISBN: 978-0-8222-2400-6

★ **REASONS TO BE PRETTY by Neil LaBute.** Greg really, truly adores his girlfriend, Steph. Unfortunately, he also thinks she has a few physical imperfections, and when he mentions them, all hell breaks loose. "Tight, tense and emotionally true." *–Time Magazine.* "Lively and compulsively watchable." *–The Record.* [2M, 2W] ISBN: 978-0-8222-2394-8

★ **OPUS by Michael Hollinger.** With only a few days to rehearse a grueling Beethoven masterpiece, a world-class string quartet struggles to prepare their highest-profile performance ever—a televised ceremony at the White House. "Intimate, intense and profoundly moving." *–Time Out.* "Worthy of scores of bravissimos." *–BroadwayWorld.com.* [4M, 1W] ISBN: 978-0-8222-2363-4

★ **BECKY SHAW by Gina Gionfriddo.** When an evening calculated to bring happiness takes a dark turn, crisis and comedy ensue in this wickedly funny play that asks what we owe the people we love and the strangers who land on our doorstep. "As engrossing as it is ferociously funny." *–NY Times.* "Gionfriddo is some kind of genius." *–Variety.* [2M, 3W] ISBN: 978-0-8222-2402-0

★ **KICKING A DEAD HORSE by Sam Shepard.** Hobart Struther's horse has just dropped dead. In an eighty-minute monologue, he discusses what path brought him here in the first place, the fate of his marriage, his career, politics and eventually the nature of the universe. "Deeply instinctual and intuitive." *–NY Times.* "The brilliance is in the infinite reverberations Shepard extracts from his simple metaphor." *–TheaterMania.* [1M, 1W] ISBN: 978-0-8222-2336-8

DRAMATISTS PLAY SERVICE, INC.
440 Park Avenue South, New York, NY 10016 212-683-8960 Fax 212-213-1539
postmaster@dramatists.com www.dramatists.com

NEW PLAYS

★ **AUGUST: OSAGE COUNTY by Tracy Letts.** WINNER OF THE 2008 PULITZER PRIZE AND TONY AWARD. When the large Weston family reunites after Dad disappears, their Oklahoma homestead explodes in a maelstrom of repressed truths and unsettling secrets. "Fiercely funny and bitingly sad." –*NY Times.* "Ferociously entertaining." –*Variety.* "A hugely ambitious, highly combustible saga." –*NY Daily News.* [6M, 7W] ISBN: 978-0-8222-2300-9

★ **RUINED by Lynn Nottage.** WINNER OF THE 2009 PULITZER PRIZE. Set in a small mining town in Democratic Republic of Congo, RUINED is a haunting, probing work about the resilience of the human spirit during times of war. "A full-immersion drama of shocking complexity and moral ambiguity." –*Variety.* "Sincere, passionate, courageous." –*Chicago Tribune.* [8M, 4W] ISBN: 978-0-8222-2390-0

★ **GOD OF CARNAGE by Yasmina Reza, translated by Christopher Hampton.** WINNER OF THE 2009 TONY AWARD. A playground altercation between boys brings together their Brooklyn parents, leaving the couples in tatters as the rum flows and tensions explode. "Satisfyingly primitive entertainment." –*NY Times.* "Elegant, acerbic, entertainingly fueled on pure bile." –*Variety.* [2M, 2W] ISBN: 978-0-8222-2399-3

★ **THE SEAFARER by Conor McPherson.** Sharky has returned to Dublin to look after his irascible, aging brother. Old drinking buddies Ivan and Nicky are holed up at the house too, hoping to play some cards. But with the arrival of a stranger from the distant past, the stakes are raised ever higher. "Dark and enthralling Christmas fable." –*NY Times.* "A timeless classic." –*Hollywood Reporter.* [5M] ISBN: 978-0-8222-2284-2

★ **THE NEW CENTURY by Paul Rudnick.** When the playwright is Paul Rudnick, expectations are geared for a play both hilarious and smart, and this provocative and outrageous comedy is no exception. "The one-liners fly like rockets." –*NY Times.* "The funniest playwright around." –*Journal News.* [2M, 3W] ISBN: 978-0-8222-2315-3

★ **SHIPWRECKED! AN ENTERTAINMENT—THE AMAZING ADVENTURES OF LOUIS DE ROUGEMONT (AS TOLD BY HIMSELF) by Donald Margulies.** The amazing story of bravery, survival and celebrity that left nineteenth-century England spellbound. Dare to be whisked away. "A deft, literate narrative." –*LA Times.* "Springs to life like a theatrical pop-up book." –*NY Times.* [2M, 1W] ISBN: 978-0-8222-2341-2

DRAMATISTS PLAY SERVICE, INC.
440 Park Avenue South, New York, NY 10016 212-683-8960 Fax 212-213-1539
postmaster@dramatists.com www.dramatists.com